GORDON W. ALLPORT, *Professor of Psychology at Harvard University and Chairman of the University's Department of Psychology is a member of Christ Church, Cambridge. He has been teacher at Robert College, Istanbul, Turkey, and at Dartmouth College. He is past president of the American Psychological Association and of the Eastern Psychological Association. Among the books of which he is author is* Personality: a Psychological Interpretation. *He is co-author of* Studies in Expressive Movement *and* The Psychology of Radio. *Mr. Allport is now serving on the Editorial Board of* The Advent Papers, *issued by The Church of the Advent, Boston, Massachusetts.*

The Roots of Religion

A dialogue between Harry Holworthy, Junior in College and his professor of psychology, Andrew Allen. The scene is the professor's office; the occasion, a conference to discuss Harry's term paper—a psychological autobiography, written for Allen's course, The Development of the Normal Personality.

ALLEN: Won't you sit down? Have a smoke?—I've been reading your term paper, and find it interesting. What you say about not getting on well with your father, about feeling inferior at athletics, and being so self-conscious, and not regarding college as close enough to life, and not finding any values that you can take seriously, and being cynical and sometimes depressed—all very interesting. And then, the pages and pages you devote to your sex life: such pre-occupation, such worries, and such candor. It shows that you feel all tangled up, and yet that you can express yourself with very few inhibitions.

HARRY: Well, you know, I found it very interesting to talk about myself once I got started. Don't you think my life's an unusual mess, Professor? Do I need psychotherapy or something? Do you think I'm neurotic?

ALLEN: Oh, I don't know. You sound much like the Great American Boy to me. I have to be careful of these term papers. If I ever shuffled them together I'd never be able to sort them out. Each one reads so much like all the rest. Yet, nearly all you fellows regard yourselves as more introverted, more anxious, more inferior, than all the others, and you all complain that life doesn't make a great deal of sense. You don't realize how much alike you are, having the same worries about yourselves, and being perplexed about politics and the war, and hoping vaguely that the Army or Navy will somehow solve all your problems for you when you get in.

TROUBLE: THE FOCUS OF AUTOBIOGRAPHY

HARRY: Maybe I do take myself too seriously. I didn't know I was so much like the other fellows. But don't we have to take ourselves seriously? What else is there these days that makes any sense?

ALLEN: Of course, we have to take our own troubles seriously. If we don't, nobody else will. Trouble is the focus of every autobiography. Everyone has his pet pains and fears to contend with, and I have come to feel that no personality is entirely normal nor mature until one's sufferings are secured in some long-range perspective. That is what I find lacking in your biography and in the autobiographies of nearly all students: the perspective that gives the stamp of maturity to personality.

HARRY: How do you mean?

ALLEN: I mean specifically that given his whole life to write about, with no restrictions whatever, only about one student in ten will mention anything in his personal document about his religious life. Can you perhaps tell me why that is so?

HARRY: Well, I never thought particularly about the subject while I was writing. Religion did come up once or twice but I left it out.

ALLEN: Why did you?

HARRY: I'll tell you frankly. I thought psychologists were beyond taking religion seriously. Didn't I read somewhere the statement that "the loss of the soul is one of the chief points of pride in the science of the soul"?

ALLEN: Probably you did; it's a telling paradox.

QUESTIONS A PSYCHOLOGIST CANNOT ANSWER

HARRY: And didn't a psychologist by the name of Leuba show some years ago that less than half of the physical scientists believed in the God of the Christian Church, and a still smaller percentage of psychologists? If I remember rightly, among the most prominent psychologists then living, only thirteen per cent said they believed in the Christian God, and only eight per cent believed in immortality.

ALLEN: I think your memory is accurate. And I don't suppose the ratio has changed greatly in the past thirty years, even though there is recently a rise of interest among psychologists in religious phenomena.

HARRY: Well, I wouldn't expect a psychologist who knows all about the workings of the human mind to accept anything anyone says about his religion. He'd see through the fantasies and rationalizations. For my part I've come to see what an illusion it all is.

ALLEN: We'd better correct one statement you just made. You say psychologists know *all* about the workings of the human mind. Actually they know very little; and Leuba's disbelievers knew very little. As a matter of fact, there's not one single basic question concerning the human mind that psychologists can answer. Where did it come from? Psychologists do not know. How is it related to our nerves and muscles, and to the material world? Even this fundamental question we cannot answer. Where is mind going when the body dies? The psychologist doesn't know. Most important of all, what ought we do with our minds now that we have them? Again, psychologists haven't a word to say.

HARRY: You mean that so far as these basic questions are concerned we might as well believe theological dogma and let it go at that?

ALLEN: I mean, where psychologists are ignorant, and in all likelihood will remain ignorant, there is no logic in following what seems to be their collective prejudice against religion.

HARRY: Well, if they are so ignorant, why do they tend not only to disbelieve, but to disparage religion? You can't say they don't. Take Freud, or take that young instructor—

DEBUNKING, AN INEXPENSIVE DIVERSION

ALLEN: I know. Having a nickle's worth of knowledge, some psychologists are willing to spend it lavishly. Many invest it in shocks and surprises that gain them attention. Debunking is an inexpensive diversion.

HARRY: But isn't it natural? Even though they may not know any fundamental answers they do know a thing or two about wishful thinking, and about sex symbolism, and about escape mechanisms. They know about the psychological roots of religion. . . . Come to think about it, I recall a neat syllogism which I made in my notes after reading Leuba. It strikes me as good reasoning:

Major Premise: God in any knowable sense can exist only in human experience, and through human inference;

Minor Premise: All human experience and human inference are subject matter for psychology;

Conclusion: Therefore, God in any intelligible sense is exclusively a psychological phenomenon.

ALLEN: Good! You've got the argument down pat. It says that the moment we have any consciousness whatsoever of God, or any thoughts of Him, not to speak of any joy, consolation, inner radiance, or awe, we make of Him an empirical God, and as such He becomes a *datum* for psy-

chology and for psychology only. A purely metaphysical
God, it is admitted, would be inaccessible to psychological
science, but such a God is not the God people think about.
As soon as any experience of Him is claimed, the entire
question becomes at once psychological.

HARRY: Well, what's wrong with that? It seems to me per-
fectly logical, and does away once and for all with the
possibility of taking religion seriously; as anything objec-
tively valid, I mean.

PSYCHOLOGISTS DO NOT GO FAR ENOUGH

ALLEN: We've stated pretty clearly certain premises of what
is called the naturalistic view of religion. Although meta-
physicians have attacked it fiercely, it has much to be said
for it. Let's follow it for a while, because I happen to believe that for intellectual people like yourself the naturalistic road is the most congenial one to travel. The trouble
is that most psychologists·who have travelled it, don't go
down it far enough. They get tired half way, and then
sit down and write a book, as Leuba and Freud, and scores
of others have done. Some, like James and Thouless, have
gone far enough to glimpse a point of convergence where
the naturalistic road and the supernatural seem to meet.

HARRY: Let's go. I've attended a lot of bull sessions on religion, but none with a psych prof before.

ALLEN: Then we'll start with a handful of simple facts that
I think no one can doubt. They are all empirical facts of

a natural order. Let's say they constitute some of the psychological roots of religion.

SOME OF THE ROOTS OF RELIGION

We know that people get their first ideas of God in childhood, and that these ideas are always twisted by the child to fit his own pint-sized mind. Many children confuse God with Santa Claus, some think their father is God. One boy thought an onrushing locomotive was God.

HARRY: You know when I was a kid I lived on a farm. My mother told me God was high and bright. For quite a while I went around thinking that the weather vane on the barn was God, because it was the highest and brightest thing I knew.

ALLEN: That's a good illustration for my point. Children, and adults too for that matter, think in terms of their own experience. What other terms can they think in? Remember, we're leaving out for the time being the hypothesis of divine revelation. Even the saints, and Christ Himself, continually represented what to them were religious realities in homely analogies. The parables, beautifully chosen as they are, are constructions out of everyday experience of the same type as your first idea of God. The Kingdom of God is like unto a mustard seed; God is like unto a weather vane. . . .

HARRY: Heaven is a place of palms and harps and wings.

ALLEN: Precisely. Those traditional images preserve for us

9

the limitations of St. John the Revelator's human experience. In his day palms were given to conquerors, harps were the loveliest musical instruments he ever heard, and a bird's wings were the fastest means of movement.

HARRY: Aren't a lot of sex symbols mixed up in religious worship?

ALLEN: Wouldn't it be extraordinary if there weren't? Creation and procreation are linked, and sex is one of the most urgent of human experiences. Wouldn't anyone, excepting Queen Victoria, be likely to draw some religious images from the sexual sphere, just as from the sphere of nourishment: the land of milk and honey, the Bread of Life? Our little store of human experience is all we have to symbolize great thoughts we are trying to express. Food and love and security and sex must all be drawn on; for religious thinking, like other kinds of thinking, proceeds in terms of analogy.

HARRY: What bothers me is the way people run to religion just as soon as they get scared. "There are no atheists in foxholes," you know, and all that. When I was a kid I was left alone one afternoon in the house and for some reason I was scared blue. I remember that I prayed and prayed and promised all sorts of favors to the Almighty if He would protect me.

ALLEN: Why not? Fear is undoubtedly one of the chief psychological roots of belief in the supernatural.

HARRY: But it seems to me that all these earthy roots just show that religion is nothing but a rationalization of human emotions, a fantasy to explain why we feel as we do. Freud calls it the Great Illusion. For example, don't you think that St. Paul's conversion might have been an epileptic fit with hallucinations?

ALLEN: It's quite possible, but did you ever stop to think that an epileptic fit might be the best avenue to the discovery of truth? And that we'd all be better off if we had more fits? The ancients suspected as much when they called epilepsy the divine disease.

HARRY: Are you trying to say that we'd all be better off if we were more abnormal?

THE ROOTS DO NOT INVALIDATE THE FRUITS

ALLEN: I'm trying to say that the psychological roots of religion have nothing to do with the validity of religious experience. Take an example from philosophy. Kant, you know, was a rationalist. Now a psychologist might point out that having a sunken chest and poor physical stamina, he was a failure physically and had few fundamental emotional satisfactions in life. Partly as a consequence, therefore, he evolved his famous doctrine of "pure reason," and said that emotions were nothing but "diseases of the intellect."

Here, let us say, was the psychological root of Kant's philosophy, but still he might have been quite correct in his conclusion. Perhaps rationalism is the truest philosophy, even though it takes an inferiority feeling like Kant's to produce the insight.

Or, take the example of George Fox, the founder of Quakerism, who was apparently psychopathic. Certainly he was eccentric, had visions, heard voices. But his powerful, if erratic personality, has affected countless lives favorably. To be specific, think of the Friends Service Committee and all that it has done to relieve human suffering. George Fox's psychopathy was one of the psychological roots of this organization, but the value of the Friends Service Committee to mankind has nothing whatsoever to do with Fox's queerness.

HARRY: Sounds like what they called pragmatism in my philosophy course.

ALLEN: Perhaps it does. But pragmatism is only the first step forward out of the muddle we were in. Many naturalists keep their eyes glued on the glands and nerves and passions and neuroses that are the matrix of human nature, and they never see what grows out of this matrix. No working of the human mind is adequately characterized by describing its roots. The flower, the fruit, and the influence of a mental condition on its possessor and on other people are parts of the story of that mental condition.

HARRY: Your point is that naturalists being preoccupied with the roots of the mind ignore the fruits of the mind?

ALLEN: Yes, or put it this way. If they are so bent on dis-

closing causes let them disclose causes all along the line.
Many psychologists have shown the effect of fear upon
the development of man's religious nature, but few have
commented on the effect of the religious outlook upon
man's fear. If we define in terms of causation we'll have
to say that religion is, in part, what grows out of human
anxiety; it is also, in part, what abolishes human anxiety.

HARRY: Would you say religion is like a good bridge? If it
holds up and does its job no one can disparage it just because the engineer who designed it had some fear or ob-
session or complex.

ALLEN: Yes, as a matter of fact, if the engineer was neu-
rotically sensitive and cautious the bridge might endure
all the better for it. I do not mean to imply that all neuroses are so benign in their effects. Many of them are
vicious and crippling. But the point is that the existence
of a neurosis in a given mind does not in itself invalidate
that mind's religious thinking.

HARRY: I'm still worried about religious symbols. There
seem to be more of them than are strictly necessary, espe-
cially in a liturgical Church. What are they good for?

ALLEN: Well, you'll agree that some symbols are necessary
both for communication and expression of thoughts and
feelings. To express or communicate the religious striving we are forced to use analogies all along the way. The
imagery of hymns is an interesting study in this connec-
tion. So, too, is *The Book of Common Prayer*. Take the

Prayer of Humble Access which contains the phrase, "We are not worthy so much as to gather up the crumbs under thy Table." What a simple domestic image this is, but what a large thought and emotion it tries to express. William James put the matter in this way, "Religious language clothes itself with such poor symbols as our life affords."

.

THE CRUX OF RELIGION

HARRY: But what is it that is being symbolized? You spoke a moment ago of "the religious striving." Seems to me that is the center of our whole problem. Just what is the religious striving?

ALLEN: Still approaching the subject naturalistically, I should say that the root of the religious striving lies in the fact that people always try to do things far in excess of their capacities.

HARRY: I don't quite get your point.

ALLEN: Let's put it this way then: the human mind has the marvelous property of soaring way off miles beyond its own competence. For example, at the present moment, we are not able to achieve peace, or a world government, or a decent social order; but that inability doesn't prevent us from purposing a solution, working for it, and appointing innumerable committees to focus, and if possible achieve, our hopes and aspirations.

HARRY: Just what has that to do with religion?

ALLEN: It's the crux of the whole matter. Religious people
in their religious moments are trying to get a satisfying
solution to the persistent emotional and intellectual riddles
that confront them. The human mind can hope for, and
envision, a lot more than it can accomplish or contain.

HARRY: Freud says somewhere that religious experience is
a sort of "oceanic feeling." Is that what you mean?

ALLEN: It is often "oceanic" enough. One sometimes feels
a vague surging and longing without one's ideas taking a
definite form or shape. Here is something H. G. Wells
once wrote—and he is not ordinarily considered to be a
religious person: "At times, in the silence of the night and
in rare lonely moments, I come upon a sort of communion
of myself and something great that is not myself. It is
perhaps poverty of mind and language that obliges me to
say that this universal scheme takes on the effect of a sympathetic person and my communion a quality of fearless
worship. These moments happen, and they are the su-
preme fact of my religious life to me; they are the crown
of my religious experiences." Note that Wells writes this
passage, as he writes everything, from the naturalistic
point of view.

HARRY: I remember once a few years ago I had gone for a
walk alone and came to the top of a hill. It was a beautiful
day, and I stretched out my arms, and had a most inde-
scribable feeling of fullness and completeness. I remem-

ber I said out loud something that sounds foolish now. I said, "I know all, I see all, I am all."

ALLEN: That was a typical mystical experience. And it is one of the forms that religious consciousness takes. It signifies a longing to have a completely unifying explanation of everything that lies inside the scope of your own life, and everything that lies beyond, which you can now only vaguely imagine.

RELIGION: THE QUEST FOR UNITY

HARRY: Could you say, in terms of certain of the German philosophers and psychologists, that one is religious when one's mind intends complete unity?

ALLEN: Yes, I like the theory of intention. It plays a big part in historical religions and it is sound psychology. The mind is always intending something; it is characteristically stretching to include more than it can. When it stretches vigorously to include all that lies within personal experience and all that lies beyond, we have a true religious attitude.

HARRY: *Re-ligio* means to bind, doesn't it? Are people religious because they want to be whole, and not so scattered? Would you say then that religion is always a "quest for unity in a disordered life"?

ALLEN: That, I think, is the kernel of the matter.

HARRY: But in actual religious activity we do not always find this "intention of unity" uppermost, do we?

ALLEN: No. It is usually present as an undercurrent, however, and in the more mystical forms of worship it predominates. But, you are right, the conscious longing for unity is only one form that religious experience takes. Sometimes it is more related to specific needs of the moment. In prayer, for example, intention usually arises from some one aspect of a person's sense of incompleteness. For example, no human being can ever love or be loved enough. He always wants more love, and so prayer and worship often stress love. At other times, fear has the upper hand, and one prays to understand or be relieved from this fear. His mind intends a solution of a particular problem, even if it cannot readily produce one. Prayers, we may say, give vent to aspiration or longing in terms of the need that is uppermost at the time.

DIFFERENCES IN RELIGION

HARRY: That would explain why religious practice takes so many forms, and why different people, having different needs, go at the matter from different points of view.

ALLEN: Yes, and here is where tolerance and understanding are needed. Before condemning a religous practice we must weigh the intention behind it. The poor juggler of Notre Dame who practiced his art before the shrine of the Virgin was symbolizing in the best way he could his purely religious intention. Even the oddest of heathen practices often makes sense if one takes pains to appreciate the intention behind them.

HARRY: From this point of view could we ever criticize any religious practice at all?

ALLEN: Only I think if the intention is somehow perverted or absent or hypocritical. When a symbol loses its finalistic intent, and for example, takes on a merely social or prestigeful intent, it is no longer religious and should be exposed. Some years ago a reporter on a Boston paper wrote that a certain clergyman gave "the most eloquent prayer ever addressed to a Boston audience." Here is a typical and frequent perversion of the religious attitude. Or, if music is taken merely for its aesthetic effect rather than as a device to facilitate the outward reaching of the mind, it is not a religious symbol. In principle, it seems to me that Protestantism often suffers a displacement of the religious attitude by the social, aesthetic, or economic attitude.

HARRY: Don't people who belong to the same Church have different conceptions of the nature of God?

ALLEN: They do, and what is more each may change his conception from moment to moment. On one occasion or in one context, God is considered omnipotent, in another, omniscient; or the loving Father, or the Giver of good gifts, or the Beautiful, the Harmonious, or the *Actus Purus*. These varied conceptions are natural enough. They come to light according to the direction of our intention at the moment. Sometimes when we stretch our minds religiously it is for the purpose of supplementing our limited strength, sometimes to supplement our limited love, sometimes to obtain more understanding, or to escape our feelings of guilt, or to find more beauty, or more peace of mind. One might say that religious practice is the flowering of all our various desires and their intended fulfillment.

RELIGION: A NORMAL ACTIVITY

HARRY: You've given me two ideas I want to think about. One is that religion somehow has more to do with the fruits of mental life than with its roots, and somehow has more to do with the intent of the mind than with its content. These two points seem to make religion a respectable and normal activity of the human mind. You'd say, I suppose, that every man, from your way of looking at it, is to some degree inescapably religious.

ALLEN: Yes, I would. Every man at least at moments intends a perfection of his own nature, a completion of his own limited being. He imagines a kind of future where a harmony is achieved and the riddles he encounters are explained. It sometimes seems that the only really clean aspect of human nature is this ability it has to intend its own perfection.

HARRY: But if religion is a clean and normal part of life, why is it that psychopaths have so many mixed-up religious thoughts?

19

ALLEN: Paranoid religious states, or what we sometimes call theopathic conditions, are really the necessary corollary of what we have been saying. A person who has had a bad breakdown is naturally disoriented: he feels strange and mysterious. What is more natural than that he should resort to religious language to explain to himself his mysterious feelings? We cannot argue from this fact that pre-occupation with religion is the cause of breakdowns; rather, just the reverse, that a disintegrating life grasps wildly at some support, and that this support becomes an odd mixture of religious ideas and personal delusions.

HARRY: Don't Jung and Freud make opposite interpretations of the relation of religion to mental breakdowns?

ALLEN: Yes, Jung's approach is closely in line with what I have been saying. He claims that side by side with the decline of the religious life comes an increase in the neuroses. His famous remark is that of thousands of patients over thirty-five years of age, "all have been people whose problem in the last resort was that of finding a religious outlook on life." To put the point in our terms, Jung argues that an adequately comprehensive "intention" is needed for normal maturity in the personality.

HARRY: And Freud?

ALLEN: Freud is one of those writers who sits down in a puddle before he has gone far enough down the road of naturalism. He calls religion a "great illusion" which is a remark on the same level as statements to the effect that it is "the opiate of the people," or a sublimation of sex, or an expression of fear. The fallacy lies in fixing attention only on certain selected roots and never considering the fruits, and in confusing the content that sometimes gets into religious consciousness with the intent that is the essence of religion.

CHRISTIANITY'S FULLNESS AND ADEQUACY

HARRY: Up to now, I assume, we've been talking about the essence of religion, without special reference to Christianity.

ALLEN: Yes, first one has to prepare a psychological groundwork for a sympathetic approach to all religion. Unless one has respect for the religious impulse wherever it is found, I don't think one can appreciate the extraordinary fullness and adequacy of historic Christianity.

HARRY: You seem to regard it as the best of all possible religions. Why is that?

ALLEN: Briefly, because it has everything. For the theoretical mind it can accommodate all that science can discover and still challenge science to dig deeper and deeper. For the social mind, it contains the highroad to all successful and just social relations, even the solution to the problems of war. For the aesthetic mind, it gives the absolutely satisfying conception of harmony and beauty. For economic and political minds, it gives a meaning to production and to power, and a guide to conduct. Its goals and ideals are always miles ahead of what any human being can fully achieve. Christianity can never cloy, because even for the most saintly Christian perfection lies ahead. The saint pursues his goal all his life long, but never attains it. Christian objectives are too high to make complete achievement possible.

HARRY: Why do you put so much stress on the unattainability of Christian ideals?

ALLEN: For the very good reason that unending, single-minded striving is in this life the one and only condition of normality in personal development. Striving is what creates unity and health in the individual. Did you ever stop to think how completely you would go to pieces if you ever obtained everything you wanted?

HARRY: Isn't that idea the theme of Goethe's *Faust?*

ALLEN: Yes, you remember what the choir of angels sings:
He who striving ceaselessly bestirs himself,
Him can we save.
According to his pact with the Devil, Faust would have been damned if he had said, *Hold, thou art so fair,* that is, if he had ever thought his goals were attained. To be a complete man is what Faust wanted, and to be a complete man he had to aspire and plan and work and reach forever toward something that lay always ahead.

HARRY: Your point is that Christianity contains all the worth-while goals that men ever strive for?

ALLEN: That is my view. The Christian philosophy of life is conducive to mental health because as a religion of striving, it has adequate comprehensiveness of goals. It catches up and focuses all the human intentions that experience convinces us are worthy of preservation.

CHRISTIANITY: SOLUTION TO THE PROBLEM OF GOOD

HARRY: And what about human intentions that are evil? Why doesn't Christianity act as a magnet for the hateful and greedy intentions that men have?

ALLEN: Because its standards are rigidly selective. It tells what sin is and the remedy for it. If it does not clearly solve the problem of evil, it at least makes it possible for mankind to live with it. No other religion seems to do so with anything like a similar measure of success. I might add that perhaps the reason Christianity helps us to get around the problem of evil so well is that it completely solves the problem of Good.

HARRY: How do you mean?

ALLEN: Its central doctrine is that of the Incarnation. Men can see in the person of Christ in concrete terms what absolute Goodness is like. His way of life and of thinking provides a tangible model for men to follow.

HARRY: But now, when you bring up the Incarnation aren't you jumping out of the natural or psychological frame of discourse into the realm of blind faith?

23

ALLEN: I'm not sure that I am. Of course there are other types of arguments to support the doctrine, but even ordinary operations of the human mind carry us a long way toward its acceptance. The elementary logic of sufficient cause compels us to accept the Incarnation, for what else could Christ, the perfect Model, be, excepting God, or as our symbolism has it, the Son of God? We know that ordinary men, even the best of them, only approximate in slight degree such perfection.

HARRY: I certainly never thought of the dogma of the Incarnation as a matter of simple logic. You say that the mind stretches toward Something, and then, lo and behold, that Something is right there in the midst of men. So that in the human realm, so to speak, we find a perfect fulfillment of all that men desire.

ALLEN: The Model does exist in the human realm, but it exists also in the divine realm. For in the person of Christ everything in humanity that is good is fulfilled and everything that is evil, that disintegrates and limits our natures, is overcome. Christ Himself said, "He that hath seen me hath seen the Father." What other conception of the Divine is possible than just this?

HARRY: You make it seem that psychology and logical thinking taken together carry us inevitably into historic Christianity. But earlier you said this road converges somewhere with the supernatural approach. I suppose you mean that psychology doesn't have anything to say about the Realities that the religious attitude implies. Does mere intention by itself guarantee that there is anything beyond?

ALLEN: Of course psychological analysis stops somewhere and faith begins. But the break is not violent, nor does it imply any serious contradictions. Let's take just one example, asking ourselves this question: Does man aspire all by himself, unaided and undirected by what theologians call the Holy Spirit? Or, as man reaches out his hand, does God reach out His, and thus intervene in the psychological series of events?

HARRY: That certainly is the question. I doubt that the average man will be satisfied to be told that he is "directionally intended" toward God. He wants to feel that God is there.

ALLEN: And there is no reason why he shouldn't. Doesn't the very fact of his striving imply a sufficient cause for the striving? Royce in his *World and the Individual* makes the case for supposing that self-consistent fragments of religious experience of necessity imply a befitting context. Now we see as through a glass darkly, and we prophesy in part. Because this partialness seems fulfilled in the course of religious striving, men are convinced that clarity and completeness exist somewhere beyond their immediate vision. . . . You see this additional step in faith is not very great. Many philosophers regard it as a necessary step. An act of faith merely completes our natural intention. Astronomers seeking a new planet have a similar faith, so do chemists seeking a new element; just so does the religious man seeking what seems to him the inevitable implication of his experiences to date. Of all the available hypotheses he finds the Christian view of life best subsumes all his observations and experiences.

HARRY: Would you approach all the so-called mysteries of the Christian faith by saying that they are a necessary complement to our own partial experience?

ALLEN: Yes, they are the reciprocal of our own limited natures. Without baptism and absolution our desire to improve our lives would not be adequately focused. Without holy matrimony the desire to make the most of our conjugal love would be unfulfilled. Without the Holy Communion we would find it difficult to acknowledge or remember adequately the Model and Master we have chosen in our lives.

HARRY: I begin to see what you mean. Beyond our own powers, we accept what more we need in order to improve our vision and complete our natures.

ALLEN: You put it well. . . . But remember, our conversation has taken the naturalistic road. We must not forget that there are all kinds of men. Some prefer to surrender their intellectual efforts early and to take more on faith. Some would find our line of reasoning cold and even presumptuous. But millions of mortals taking many paths have come to essentially the same conclusion. Even though no two perhaps have exactly the same conception of individual points in the Gospel or in the sacraments, still the attention of all is riveted to the picture of God taking human nature, and on the Cross exemplifying manhood perfected through the triumph of love over suffering. No model in the history of the human race compares with this. It is the central image toward which Christians address themselves, finding it always meaningful and always satisfying. Some, I admit, see the Crucifixion as a one-time distant event, and fail to realize its significance for men's struggles today. But the more discerning find the event of present importance, seeing how day by day men crucify the good within them, and day by day the good within rebukes, forgives, and restores.

HARRY: Can you tell me why it is that some people are more religious than others? From what you say I should think that everyone would have about the same needs, the same intentions, and would reach the same satisfying conclusions.

ALLEN: I'm not going to attempt to answer that question. The problem, I admit, puzzles me too. Before I can make up my own mind I'd like to investigate further. If we had adequate religious autobiographies from people who are religious, and from people who are irreligious, we'd know better why human minds differ in this respect.

HARRY: Well, I'd be glad, now that we've had our talk, to write you the full story of my own religious life, such as it is. . . . But you haven't yet told me whether you think

I need some kind of psychotherapy. Don't forget I have
my personal problems.

ALLEN: I predict that your religious autobiography, when
it is completed, will be therapy enough. But don't hurry
with it. Live it before you write it.

THE PATTERN OF A RELIGIOUS AUTOBIOGRAPHY

HARRY: What do you suppose it will look like?

ALLEN: You've already told me enough about yourself to
permit me some guesses. I suppose it will start with an
account of how, as a child, you accepted unquestioningly
the religious content taught by your parents and by
the Sunday school you attended. Then will come the story
of juvenile doubts about the literal adequacy of this content. When you began to study elementary psychology
you felt that what remained of the imagery, symbols, and
dogma were blown sky high. Then came, as in every life,
frustrations, inferiority, new fears, and suffering. These
emotions you found almost too much to bear. At the same
time you had a longing to find some explanation for the
maladies and a remedy. Your mind hopped ahead, imag-
ining this solution or that, always bent on saving itself
from disintegration. Half-consciously your childhood
teachings lingered on, but you knew they would have to
be entirely overhauled, changed, expanded so that they
might be, not second-hand, but first-hand fittings to your
personality. Only by degrees did it dawn on you that historic Christianity held the complement to your nature and

a fulfillment of your needs. Like some people you may find as the first stage a growing conviction that Christianity holds the only solution to social questions. Nowadays, we read this statement more and more frequently, because momentarily human needs are greatest in this direction. Or you may find in historic Christian practice that your restlessness is stilled, or your craving for beauty is supplied, or your feelings of guilt allayed. I cannot tell what steps it may take. No two histories are alike But the quest once begun never ends, even though the goal you seek becomes more and more certain. Having once experienced the blessedness of certainty, even though but for a moment, you will never be satisfied, but will be impelled to seek to regain and extend this experience all your life long.

HARRY: You size me up pretty boldly—but maybe correctly too; I cannot yet say. Will you tell me where the therapy comes in? You see I'm still worried about myself.

ALLEN: You will find therapy as a by-product of your religious quest. Anyone who sets out in a self-indulgent manner to find a cure for his inner ailments is likely to fail in finding it. The person who directs his attention to his religious quest usually finds therapy along the way—unexpectedly.

HARRY: In a vague sort of way I've known all along that what you've just been saying is probably right. But it's not too easy to follow this road.

ALLEN: I know: it's much easier to sit down in the puddle
and howl for help. But you're not the type that does it.

HARRY: Thanks for thinking so. There are a lot of people
I admire and a lot that I don't admire, and you've given
me a clue to the difference between them. Some squawk
for assistance when they run into personal trouble; the
others have some sort of inner poise that I never before
quite understood. I think I do now begin to understand
it. They've made some progress in their religious quest.

ALLEN: I hope you see why I did not regard your autobiography as complete. Write me another chapter in five
years; will you?

HARRY: I certainly will. I've got more thinking to do first,
and maybe some more suffering. . . . I wonder if anyone's
religious ideas can be mature before he is twenty-five or
thirty years old. . . . Then if they aren't mature by thirty-
five, maybe he'll suffer the consequences as did Jung's
patients. . . . Well, I've got a few more years to go. . . .
Anyway, you've given me something to mull over. . . .
Thanks a lot.

ALLEN: Goodbye, Harry. Keep your mind on that chapter

9 780344 980305